Consent Based Parenting

How to raise children in charge of their own bodies

By

Abby Norman

For my mom and dad:

Thanks for raising me right.

Introduction

What do you know about parenting? I wonder that a lot lately. I currently have a three and four year old at home, which means I had a two year old and three year old at the same time. If that doesn't make you sure that you are doing the entire parenting thing wrong at least twice a day, then you are a stronger person than I.

I would be lying if I didn't tell you that I struggle as a parent some days. I yell when I shouldn't, I probably let my kids watch too much TV (Netflix makes "just one more" morph into "how have you been staring at a screen all day?" all too easily.) I have to call my husband in for back up at least daily. Toddlers are just plain hard. I am doing the best I can, aren't we all? Sometimes, the best I can is nothing to brag about.

So why write about parenting and specifically sex talks and parenting? I hang out with teenagers all day long, and have for the last eight years. I'm not a creeper. I am a high school teacher, and I have spent my entire adult life learning about what teenagers think. I teach literature, and the best way to get the stories to stick is to talk about what the students think about those stories. I have learned not only what teenagers think, but also why they have come to those conclusions.

While sometimes they get it right, teens often have ideas about this world that are desperately wrong. My teenage students are confused about basic ideas like what consent is, and how to respectfully go about operating their own body in regards to other bodies. This may surprise us, but it shouldn't. Not a week goes by where some celebrity or another is in the news for saying something stupid about rape and consent, then our Facebook friends spend at least three days arguing about whether or not what the celebrity said is defensible. (Spoiler alert: It almost never is.)

With the world sending confusing messages about how to operate our bodies, it is essential as parents that our message is clear and consistent. This means coming up with a frame work that you can explain to all ages. The phrase we have latched onto in our house is this: **Everyone is in charge of their own bodies.**

Think of this phrase like a filter that you insert into your brain. You take all your thoughts and put them to the test. If the thought cannot go through the filter, then the thought should not come out of your mouth.

Like every good rule, there are of course exceptions. When a child is putting themselves in danger, they can no longer be in charge of their own bodies. Very small children need to be taught what to wear or eat or drink so they can learn how to make healthy choices. You cannot just leave a kid completely to their own devices because "Hey! They are in charge of their own bodies!" Think of this ideology instead, like a fence that you slowly expand the parameter. Within the fence, can you allow your child to be in charge of their own body?

It seems like an easy thing, but when I inserted the filter in my own head, I was surprised at how many normal thoughts and behaviors were filtered out. Regardless of the age of your children, be gentle with yourself. This might be a new parenting paradigm you are trying on; it might take a while for it to feel like it fits. Maybe your kids are older, talk to them. Tell them that you want to try out this crazy new rule. Let them help you. After all, isn't the first step in letting everyone be in charge of their own body telling them they are?

When and Where

Can I tell you a secret? Teenagers are listening to the adults in their lives a lot more than we think they are. They are really listening, and they have been for a long time. Teens will regularly quote their parents directly and tell me what their grandparents said. My students have been known to use my words against me. Y'all, this is good news. They are hearing us! Even when they pretend they are not.

But it is also scary news. Y'all they are hearing us, even when we aren't being incredibly careful about what we are telling them. Even when we are just trying to get through the day, they are hearing us. Our words and actions have consequences, so we need to make sure we are teaching consistent and correct information.

This starts way before the teenage years. Just like we don't wait until our kids start driving to talk to them about safety, seat belts, stop signs, and road rage, we shouldn't wait until puberty to talk to our kids about sex and sexual ethics. With a two year old and a three year old, it felt weird thinking about talking to them about sex. When I reframed the conversation to talking about bodies, about their bodies, and my body, suddenly it was a conversation that small children are very interested in.

I am sure I am not the only one who has children who could talk about their bodies (and their mommy and daddy's bodies) all day long. When my oldest was not even two she got a mosquito bite on her arm and announced loudly, to anyone who would listen (especially in the grocery store) that she had grown a third nipple on her arm. She was very proud of this nipple that did not hide under her shirt. And this behavior embarrassed me. I didn't want my kid yelling about her nipple in the grocery store, especially when it wasn't even a nipple!

Part of my embarrassment was thinking of nipples as sexual. They aren't to my daughter, at least not yet. They are as benign as toes or fingernails. She thinks they are as cool as her hair or her fingers. We talk about her arms and her legs at our house, we talk a lot about where her tiny hands and fingers do and do not belong. Why not talk about her nipple shaped mosquito bite too?

It is not sexual for her. Nor is your kid's obsession with his penis, or my other girl's incessant need to talk about her butt, in anyway sexual. These things are just a part of them. They want to talk about the boo-boos on their knees and their penises and vaginas and their eyes and their hair and their toes. Of course they do! We are always and forever interested in ourselves (I mean, who doesn't love a good Buzzfeed quiz about which thing you are?) and for our kids, this extends to their bodies.

I know that it is weird for us when our kids start talking about nipples in the grocery store or asking if their Sunday school teach has a vagina (while we are at church.) I know that sometimes we can't help but blush and stutter a little bit. But we have to talk to our kids on their terms. This way they know we are willing to have the conversation.

I had the sex talk with my mom in the middle of a Target parking lot. It was my first day of third grade and the teacher was going over what she was going to teach us that year. I was pretty excited about the possibility of learning where babies came from, and told my mom as such as we were pulling into the parking lot to fetch Elmer's glue and Lisa Frank folders. She pulled into a spot and looked at me. "I can tell you all about where babies come from." And she did.

I don't know if it was her plan or not. I think that talk was done in the house with both of my sisters. But for me, the Target parking lot was where I asked, so the Target parking lot was where I was answered. I don't know whether my mom was embarrassed or not. She didn't act like it. The question was put out there, and it was answered.

I know it is weird to talk about things that are, in our minds, very firmly private, in places that are semipublic. But our children don't yet see those conversations as embarrassing, and that is a good thing! We want them to ask. If they ask us we can ensure they get accurate information. I have heard the things teenagers say when they are just guessing about sex, and it is terrifying.

Encouraging the conversations with us, makes the conversations more accurate.

The other awesome thing my parents instilled in me was the ability to have these sorts of conversations about sex and the body. Because I was never taught to be embarrassed about these conversations, I just never was. I had them openly. As I began entering into the world of romantic relationships, I told boys about what I was and was not comfortable doing before we were even dating. I talked openly about my body to my parents, sisters, and doctors. I knew how to have these conversations because I had practice having them. I had, after all started having them in the Target parking lot.

Many of my friends in high school were unable to talk about sex while also choosing to be sexually active. This was both confusing and harmful to them, and I see the same things playing out with my high school students.

Children, who grow up to be teens and young adults need to have a lot of practice talking about sex and bodies in totally low stakes environments. Talking about sex and bodies with a person you are attracted to can feel scary and risky even if you are totally comfortable talking about sex. These conversations become nearly impossible when you aren't comfortable talking about sex and bodies at all. In high school I remember some of my sexually active friends being afraid to say when things hurt, or not even being sure when and where they would be having sex until a boyfriend walked into a grocery store and bought condoms. All of this was done as they sat quietly because they simply didn't know how to have conversations about sex.

This doesn't stop at high school. I know married women who can barely manage to talk about sex and their own bodies with their doctors, or with their husbands. They don't know how to ask for what they need, to say when something hurts, to say what feels good. They don't know how to tell their doctors they can't orgasm. They go into labor without knowing everything that will happen to their body because they don't want to talk about it.

I know men who would rather die than tell anyone there is something wrong with their penis, and frankly that could cause death. I know teenage boys who are just hoping their girlfriend is on birth control, but they are afraid to ask her. I know husbands who refuse to know anything about the birthing process because it is "none of their business."

All of these extremely harmful attitudes stem from our unwillingness to talk about sex and bodies except for in very sterile circumstances. Sexual and body ethics don't happen in sterile circumstances. They happen in everyday life. We are making people think that these conversations are weird and uncomfortable by refusing to have them. The only way to make these conversations safe and normal is practice. I promise, if you let them, your kids will bring bodies up. Then you just have to treat the conversation as though they are asking you about their elbow.

Our kids take our cues from us. This proves to be true when you think about dinner conversations across the country. My uncle is a dog breeder. The word "bitch" isn't shocking to anyone when he uses it at the dinner table because that is what he is talking about. It is the right name for a female dog he is breeding. While it was really weird to me that my uncle was just using that word, it took me about four minutes to get used to the idea. The same is true for funeral directors. It isn't that weird for their families to talk about death at the dinner table. Whatever you make normal, will be what your kids talk to you about.

In an age where kids can google any answer up within seconds, it is important that we become the easiest and most accessible way to the information they want. And they want information about sex and bodies. If we foster an environment where questions are answered openly and honestly, our kids won't have to go anywhere else for their information.

I know that an open sense of communication fosters open questions because my parents had it. We had a computer with internet installed when I was thirteen. My oldest sister had gone to college and my mom wanted to be able to email her oldest daughter. Besides the basic keeping the computer in a place that was accessible to everyone, my parents had no filters on the computer. I suppose I could have googled anything I wanted. (In those days I think I was using Ask Jeeves.) But I didn't need to. My mom had always answered all of my questions.

This wasn't just beneficial for me. All my friends soon found out that I could get any questions we had, answered. I became the go to for accurate information. In some ways, I still am. My students have, when they found out I am willing to answer, asked me some very confused questions. Can I get pregnant from skinny dipping? Does my pee come out the same place babies come out? Can you get AIDS from kissing? Does having a big butt mean you are easy? Does having a big butt means you have to have sex? I should never have to teach a high school girl that she isn't dying, she is simply menstruating. That conversation needs to happen well before she hits the ninth grade. Our kids are going to get the information one way or another. We need to foster an environment, far before they are asking, where they feel comfortable talking to us about their bodies.

The How

Our words are a good place to start, but everyone knows that actions speak louder than words. Here's the thing. I think sometimes we forget that our babies are people from the beginning. I don't mean to hate on social media. It is here to stay and for the most part my life has benefited from it. But social media has made the appearance of our lives increasingly more important as we share more with the world. And children are terrible at appearances.

I think sometimes we treat our kids like props to make our lives look nice on Facebook. I only know because I've been there, in fact I still struggle with this. I want my girls to wear matching outfits, to keep their clothes clean, to make messes but only cute Instagram-able ones. If my girl's autonomy is like the fence I talked about in the introduction, then I make the fence like a tiny pen they can't even turn around in simply because I want a great *looking* life.

The attitude that babies should just do what we want, simply because they are babies, is wrong. And this attitude shows up even before they do. When you are about my age, with children about my age, (and you have the sort of talk about anything attitude that I have) you end up spending whole dinner parties talking about birthing. (I know, I am sorry.) Here's the deal: Birthing is the story of two people, not one.

I am one of the lucky ones, who had babies pretty much exactly as I planned to. But even then the two experiences were totally different. My girls each came the way they were going to, and unsurprisingly, they came out according to their personalities, my more stubborn of the two coming out only after much prodding and a little threatening. Babies are people too, and the way we talk about birth needs to include a baby's autonomy. Yes, you have a plan. Yes, you went to the classes and want things to go a certain way. But if the baby refuses, that isn't anyone's fault or failing. Sometimes, it just is. Babies get to have some say in their own birth, even if we refuse to acknowledge it.

When they are infants, we need to respect our children's space as individuals. When my youngest was just a few weeks old I was still struggling with breast feeding. But I was determined. Good mom's breastfeed! Breast is best! This is natural! Meanwhile my kid was feeding every 45 minutes and I was completely losing my mind. But I had decided that I would breastfeed.

It was, as I mentioned, not going well. Through a series of events that can only be described as miraculous intervention, I ended up at the house of the best lactation consultant in the city. After watching me struggle with feeding my own baby for a while she gently touched my arm. "Abby, don't you see what your baby is trying to tell you? She is tired. You need to let her rest." My baby had a posterior tongue tie, causing her tiny mouth to work very very hard to get any milk at all. Her little body would get totally exhausted, and she would fall asleep before she was full, then wake up forty-five minutes later starving.

I didn't see any of this. Part of this was because I was a new mom and really who the heck knows what they are supposed to do anyway? But part of this was because I wasn't listening. The lactation consultant gently reminded me that there are two people in a breastfeeding relationship, the mother and the child. I had unilaterally decided what was best for everyone. I hadn't let my daughter tell me what she needed.

It is strange to think that we need to respect the autonomy of someone who cannot even support their own head, but we do. We need to practice while the baby is teeny-tiny. When you are feeding or changing or patting, tell the baby what you are about to do. Let them know when you are getting into their personal space. Don't just yank their legs up for a diaper change, tell them first. It feels silly initially, but it is important. Because if birth isn't the place you give your child autonomy, when do you start? When they talk? When they walk? When they are legally adults? If we wait till they are legal adults, then just hand them 100 percent bodily autonomy, that is like handing a kid who has never driven in his whole life a new Porsche. That 18-year-old is going to crash.

Once your kiddo starts cooing and crawling, it is time to up the stakes on autonomy. I am by no means suggesting you let your little peanut stick his finger in the light socket because that is what he wants to do. But when can you let him be in spaces that are safe for him to roam freely? Can you give her access to her toys so she can pick what you play with sometimes? How can we slowly let out the reins on being in charge of your own body, so by the time they walk out the door to go to college, or face the world, we feel like our kids are ready for it?

What if practicing degrees of personal autonomy with our babies were a natural progression, just like eating is? Of course we don't have our baby cook a steak and eat it, but by the time they are eighteen, they should know how to operate a grill. Our kids are going to college with little more than baby food of personal autonomy, then we are surprised when they hurt themselves or other people. Being in charge of your own body needs to be practiced every day, in ways that are appropriate for your child, so they are experts when it is time for them to go out on their own.

You Can Always Help It

When it comes to sex, sometimes we treat people like they are feral dogs. We get the impression that some people simply cannot help acting out of their sexual desire. This attitude comes in many forms. Some people I know refuse to be in a car or by themselves with a member of the opposite sex as to "avoid all temptation." Other people I know have different standards of behavior for boys and girls because "boys will be boys after all." I have heard all kinds of behavior excused, from hands being where they don't belong, to people having sex with someone who isn't their spouse, swept away with the phrase, "They couldn't help it."

If everyone is in charge of their own body, then everyone can always help their own behavior. While this idea is acted out most often as adults in sexual situations, this concept needs to be taught to us from a very early age. My two daughters are very close in age, and like most siblings they fight quite often. Inevitably, (and completely predictably) I often catch the person who acts out second. It is always the responder who gets caught.

This can be hard to parent. But I have stopped sussing out exactly what happened. Instead, I employ the rule taught to me by my parents: I will only speak to you about your own actions. My dad was a trained mediator and he always used this trick on his own children. While what other people did to me did matter, he would only speak to me about my own behavior, because the only behavior I was in charge of was my own.

Perhaps my older girl did hit her little sister first. (This isn't likely, but possible.) That doesn't matter in the context of talking to my younger daughter, because I am only speaking to her about her own behavior. Hitting is always inappropriate. Period. So I need to speak to her about her hitting. That is really the only behavior she can control. It is inappropriate to hit people. You need to keep your hands to yourself. You don't get to inflict unwanted touch on another person's body. It doesn't matter what that person did. I am concerned about you controlling your own behavior.

Kids need to understand they are not victims to their circumstances. They do not have to hit their sister, they do not have to yell when they are angry, and they do not have to behave sexually toward someone they are attracted to. They do not have to objectify a person because of the way that person chose to dress or move. A person always gets to be in charge of their own body, and this means that a person is always responsible for their own actions.

All the time we reinforce the idea that all people, but especially teenagers, are victims to their sexuality. Look at the way dress codes are handed down. The vast majority of high school dress codes are built so that the girls will not be "a distraction" to the boys. Right there in the rules, in the suspensions, in the discipline referrals, is the idea that the boys cannot control themselves. Boys, of course, will be unable to study or pay attention because they are victims of their own desire, they are boys, how could they help it?

These sorts of policies are harmful for boys and for girls. Boys are taught that they cannot control themselves. If something is attractive to them it is either dangerous and they should stay away from it at all costs, or it isn't their fault if they act on these desires. Do you see how harmful, this is? If we teach boys that the girls are responsible for the boys getting distracted in class, then isn't the logical extension of that rule that girls are also responsible for boys behavior outside of class? If a boy can't help looking, then how can he help touching? What if we empowered boys with the idea that they are always in control of their own body, regardless of what a person does or does not do, is or is not wearing, the boy is always able to control his own actions and treat people in a way that is kind and respectful. What if we empowered all people to believe that regardless of the way someone is acting, you have the ability to act respectfully toward that person, *even when that person is not being respectful towards themselves?*

While we teach boys they are not in control of themselves, we teach girls that their bodies are dangerous. If you wear a shirt that is too low, yoga-pants that are too tight, or shorts that show too much leg, you will hurt the boys. They will not be able to control themselves around you and this will damage them. Your body has the potential to damage other people even when you don't mean for it to. We teach girls that they are responsible for the ways that men respond to them, and this is dangerous.

I was told not to wear a pair of shorts to school in the seventh grade. I wasn't called out of class, and it was even done in a way that was meant to appear casual, but I haven't worn a pair of shorts since. I have long legs and in my teen years I could not find a pair of shorts in the girls department that fit the dress code, so I stopped buying them. I haven't worn a pair of shorts since 1998. I didn't want anyone to get hurt. I didn't anyone to get the wrong idea about me because I was exposing too much leg. I still don't wear shorts. (Though, writing this makes me aware that it is time for me to find some shorts next summer, for myself and for my girls.)

The idea that women need to be weary of their dangerous bodies is pervasive in our culture. Cover up while breast feeding, because if someone stares it is your fault. Don't dress a certain way if you don't want to get grabbed. If something terrible happens to you, what did you do to deserve it? Many rape survivors recount stories of being asked what they were wearing and doing to deserve being raped. This idea, that women are somehow responsible for being raped, needs to be stopped, and it starts well before that day. We need to stop telling our daughters that their bodies are dangerous. Girls are only responsible for their bodies, and not for the reactions of anyone else.

Instead we need to teach everyone that you are only in control of yourself, and you are always in control of yourself. You can always control your own actions, and I, as your parent will do the loving work of continually reminding you of that. I will always hold you responsible for your own behavior, regardless of what anyone else in the situation was doing.

Sex, Violence and Language

I am growing increasingly bothered by the way teenagers are talking about sex. Did you know smashing is euphemism for sex? I found this out in my classroom when I meant to say that people were using a baseball bat to beat up an old car but what I said was two people were smashing in a car. What my student's heard was that the two people were having sex in a car. Smash in a car no longer means beat in the doors. It means having sex in.

Smash isn't the only violent term for sex that is commonly used and I am not just talking about the f word. Hit that, tap her, our teens are using violent language to talk about sex, even consensual sex. Our teens think of sex as something that someone does to someone else and not something that people do together.

If sex is seen as a violent act, it can't be totally consensual, it is inherently something done to someone. Violent acts are done *to* people not *with* people. If everyone always acts in such a way so that everyone is in charge of their own body, then sex isn't violent. Period.

Kids on the playground know what is powerful. Before they even know what oral sex is, or why someone would want to do that, boys wield the phrase "suck my dick" as the ultimate power move. (I remember when the Clinton scandal happened, I was in middle school and suddenly there was a lot that needed explaining. I had already asked my parents, and they had given me the facts and their moral take on when and where this behavior was appropriate. Good thing they did, because my friends wanted to know too! I remember explaining oral sex to my friend and she was totally disgusted. Why would anyone ever want to do that?) Boys aren't saying "suck my dick" because they are desiring pleasure, they are saying it because they know it is vulgar and insulting. This is a thing that you do to me because I am in charge of you. Then the boy gets in trouble for saying it because it is vulgar and inappropriate for someone their age to be saying. The idea that you are not allowed to tell someone else what they are doing to your body is not even mentioned.

We need to shift the paradigm from, that is an inappropriate thing to say because it is rude and adult to, that is harmful because you are telling someone what they are going to do with their body and you do not get to do that. Or, you are telling people what they *will do* to your body and that is inherently violent.

Is it inappropriate for elementary school students engaging in highly sexual acts? Yes. Do we need to teach students about how they aren't ready to be engaging in this sexual behavior and how they will know they are ready? Absolutely, but kids yelling suck my dick at each other on the school bus is not in fact about sexual acts. It is about trying to shock, embarrass and control people. When kids use those sexual words and gestures as violent weapons, we need to address it as violence. You are not allowed to tell anyone else what they will do with their body or what you will do to their body without their permission, because everyone is in charge of their own body.

The same is true for the language in popular songs. The songs that refer to sex in terms of what you do to someone without their permission, or the songs that tell someone not only what will be done with their body, but then also how the person has to feel about it are wrong. These songs are often construed as being "nasty" because they talk about sex explicitly. I don't think that the explicit language is the reason they are so damaging. They are damaging because they normalize violent behavior where everyone is not in charge of their own body.

If sex is something that isn't totally mutual, suddenly it has a lot of power. If our kids talk about sex like a violent act, they are thinking about it in terms of power. What does violent sexual behavior imply about a person's sexuality? Someone's sexuality should not be acted out at the expense of someone else. Ever. But it is.

Literally every day there are stories in newspapers across the country of men acting violently because their advances are denied. Recently, I read a story of a man shooting and killing a woman because she would not go on a date with him. This is a direct result of the violent thoughts about sex.

See, the only way to be a "real man" is to act out your sexual desires onto someone else. By denying the man a date this woman was denying him his manhood. He needed to prove he was in charge of her body, so he killed her. I know that this seems extreme, but it is a natural consequence of seeing sex as violent, and if we are using language that is violent, we are thinking of sex as violent.

If everyone is in charge of their own body, suddenly the power dynamics of sex are removed and the mutuality is restored. Everyone gets to make decisions and sexuality cannot be used as a weapon. If everyone is free to advocate for themselves and everyone is ensuring that this is happening, it takes all the power dynamics out of sexual interactions, which makes it impossible for sex to be used violently.

Redefining Romance

It doesn't take that much to see how the violent ways our children are thinking about sex is problematic. But there are more subversive ways the understanding of sex as power can sneak into our understanding of the world. The ways we think and talk about romance often directly contradict the idea that everyone is in charge of their own body.

If I have learned anything from my daughters about romantic relationships, it is that our kids are exposed to romance *way* before we think they are. We can thank Disney and the princess industrial complex for that. My girls, at two and three, became obsessed with marriage. Who gets married? Why do people get married? Are you and daddy married? Are you going to get married again? (I suspect this last one is more about dancing and cake than it is about making sure we still love each other.) Their obsession with princesses has led to their obsession with marriage, and love, and how people fall in love.

Enter conversations about romance. Before our kids have feelings of romance, our stories, and especially our fairytales, show our kids how romantic relationships are supposed to be played out. I don't love the lessons these stories are teaching. In most classic fairy tales the woman does not get to be in charge of her own body.

In both Snow White and Sleeping Beauty the prince comes upon a sleeping lady, and though he barely knows her, or does not know her at all, the prince is just totally sure that he is supposed to kiss her. Let me re-iterate, she is asleep. She cannot consent to being kissed or give any indication that she wants to be kissed, but he goes ahead and kisses her. This behavior is heroic. It is the charming, valorous thing to do, to simply take charge of the situation, even if that means taking charge of someone else's body.

In Cinderella, the prince chases after a woman who has run away from him. She literally is escaping so fast she loses a shoe and does not go back for it. The prince assumes that it couldn't possibly be him that she is running from. Chasing after her makes him the hero and allows her to live happily ever after.

But don't these women *want* these men to pursue them? Isn't that the point? Yes. I suppose it is the point. And that point makes these stories even more dangerous. Not only do these stories give boys the dangerous narrative that they are entitled, and even expected to decide what a girl wants, it gives girls the idea that they should not advocate for their own needs. The truly romantic thing for a man to do is predict accurately what you want, and then give it to you. A man's desire to pursue you somehow proves your worth. And if you have to tell a man what you want, then he must not really like you.

Girls also learn that they are somehow not allowed to say what they want, especially when it comes to their bodies. After all, if you admit that you have sexual feelings, that you are longing to be held or kissed or touched by someone else, then you are needy, or a slut. Boys are supposed to have sexual feelings, but girls are supposed to avoid them. They aren't allowed to say what they want. If a boy really likes you he will anticipate your needs and meet them.
This puts boys in a confusing and dangerous position. In order to be a man you must not only meet the needs of a woman you must also figure out what those are. A real man lets a woman know what she wants. In fact, women want it this way. So, when a boy tries to pursue a girl, and she says no, what does that mean? Does that mean she really doesn't want you to talk to her, or does she want you to try harder? If it is the former, but you take it as the latter, then you wind up with a restraining order.

Fairy tales aren't the only medium giving these confusing messages. Almost every romantic comedy has some element of the man figuring out what the woman wants and then proving to her that she wants it. Many romantic songs buy into the idea that true romance is a man telling a woman what she really wants and then give it to them.

We need to put everyone in charge of their own bodies, and then teach that respect of boundaries is truly romantic. It shouldn't be lame to ask someone if they want to be hugged, kissed, or otherwise physically engaged with you. It shouldn't be shameful to have desires and be able to clearly communicate them. Being able to talk about what you are comfortable with should be a baseline for whether or not we want to date each other. It shouldn't be embarrassing to admit that you are not ready to do something, or you don't want to do it now even though you did yesterday.

Our ideas about romance are messing with our understanding of consent. What if smooth operators were people who only did things with express permission, and not people who "got away" with more than other people? I would feel much more comfortable with my kids going on dates if the standard were "awesome dates are dates where everyone is in charge of their own bodies and consent was asked for if there is any doubt." That boy/girl respects you as a person, that is so romantic.

Are You a Safe Place?

Here is the deal about kids today, they are going to get the information they are after. Just this week my three year old figured out how to operate the voice operated google function on my phone. (OK Google, picture of pigs!) Just three years old and she can get what she needs from the internet. On the one hand, this is really awesome. My kids can learn about anything that interests her! On the other hand, this is terrifying. My kid doesn't even have to be able to type to ask Google where babies come from.

In an age where our kids can google anything, how can we be the place our kids go to for information? We need to build enough trust with our kids that they trust we are a safe place to go. How do you respond when your kids ask you something? It doesn't start with sexual questions. What do you do when your kids ask you about dinosaurs, or the latest celebrity they saw on Sesame Street? How do you respond when your fourth grader gets super excited about a science project you know very little about? If you don't know something, are you willing to learn together?

Before there was Google, there was the public library. If my mother taught me anything, it was that you can learn anything you want to know if you have a library card. We learned about cake decorating, American history, art projects, anything we wanted to know really. Questions about sex and the body weren't treated any differently. My mom knew the answer, but if she didn't then she didn't shrug us off. We looked it up, we learned, our questions were answered. This extended to questions about sex and our bodies. Books were checked out, questions were answered in age appropriate ways.

Questions about what body part words meant were answered in the same tone that questions about vocabulary words were. When we accidentally said a cuss word because we didn't know it was one, we were corrected in a way that wasn't shameful. When we made a mistake about talking about our bodies we were gently corrected. It just wasn't a big deal, so we always knew it was safe to ask.

Later on my parents showed us that they were safe places to land. I know I have said it three times before, but your teens are always listening to you. What are you saying about other people in front of them? Are you treating the girl who got pregnant in her class with as much contempt as her classmates are? Are you saying how stupid your son's friend is for getting his girlfriend pregnant?

I am not suggesting that you should not be talking to your kids about consequences of actions. Of course, when a peer shows up pregnant your teens are going to want to talk about it, and you probably do too. But be careful about the words you are using. You need to be leading with grace. While yes, this person did just make a choice you want your child to avoid, there are ways to discuss this without using shame. You need to make sure your teens know that if they do get themselves in a situation that you don't love, you will still love them.

When I was in about the fourth grade one of my cousins got pregnant. She was eighteen and just graduating from high school. My mom sat us down to tell us that our cousin was pregnant, which meant she had been sexually active, something my parents didn't approve of until marriage. And in the same breathe my mom told us that she still loved her niece as much as she ever had and we would be throwing our cousin a baby shower because it is important to support the people we love. We were going to love the heck out of that baby, was that clear? Yes. It was clear, and it was also clear that our parents would love us no matter what too.

Our kids are going to act outside of what we want for them. I happen to agree with my parents, that sex is best saved for marriage. I hope my children listen to me and come to the same conclusions as they grow up, but they might not. I need to make sure that they know that I will always love them, that I will never be ashamed of who they are, even if I don't love the choices they make.

We have to be building this trust constantly, with how we treat our kids, their friends, and other people in our lives. If we are a safe place to land, giving our kids the truth and acting with grace, they won't google. They will just ask us. Answering our kids' questions is a huge responsibility, and also a great privilege. It should be treated as such.

Practicing Consent

I'm not really a theory person. I spent four years in college learning all about educational theory, only to learn I didn't know anything when I actually started teaching. All that stuff they taught me in college was about imaginary classrooms where all the kids are magically self-motivated and know the value of everything I am trying to teach them. Ha! That isn't real, which means all that learning I received for four years was also mostly useless.

I don't want this book to be useless. If you can't apply the idea that everyone is in charge of their own bodies in a way that makes sense for your families, then what good is that idea in theory? It needs to work in practice too. And I do mean practice, every day you can find ways to reinforce to kids they are in charge of their own bodies. This is, by no means, meant to be an exhaustive list. Rather, think of it as a starting off point for your family.

The bathtub is a great place to talk about consent. (Thanks to Suzanne Paul who writes at The Smitten Word for this.) Where do you want me to wash next? Do you want to wash your tummy or do you want me to wash your tummy? Okay! Time to rinse your hair. Do you want to dunk in the water, or pour with a cup?

Getting dressed is a battle zone in our house, and it is often a place where I inadvertently take away my kid's autonomy because I am just too tired to deal with it. I try really hard to always give my girls at least two choices. My youngest hates pants. So, I try to make sure that the choices I have for her are either dresses or skirts. As they get older, I really don't want to be warring over clothes all the time, but I know it is a possibility. I am not going to let them leave the house in a bikini in December, but I am going to try to not make clothes a power battle. I am hoping we can come to some basic rules and then they can dress within those boundaries as they choose.

Dinner is another time letting kids being in charge of their own bodies can be a little tricky. At my house the kids always have two choices. They can either eat what I am serving or they can request a peanut butter and jelly sandwich. As soon as they are old enough, they will be making that sandwich themselves. I know some people have stricter policies about food, and I totally respect that. For me, it isn't worth it. If you do find yourself in major food battles, try to come up with ways your kid can be in charge of their eating. Can they choose the order it all goes down the hatch? Can they eat raw carrots instead of the cooked broccoli they hate? How can you give your child the maximum amount of autonomy?

When kids are fighting, it is important that they are reminded that everyone is in charge of their own body. My girls regularly get into fights because one won't stop touching the other, or one refuses to hug the other. It is important for me to reinforce that everyone is in charge of their own body by not making my kids hug or kiss when they don't want to. And I never tell a kid who is being touched when she does not want to be to ignore it. I try to negotiate these fights so that everyone is in charge of what happens to their own bodies.

When you visit relatives sometimes things get tricky. We live far away from a lot of our relatives. This means when my kids are toddlers, they often do not know or remember seeing a relative who may fully expect a hug or a kiss. I think it is really important we don't make our kids engage in physical contact they aren't comfortable with. If they don't want to give a hug hello, I simply tell the relative that. It hasn't always been totally accepted, but this is something I feel strongly about. I want my kids to know that they don't have to give physical affection they aren't comfortable with.

Bed time is another place I like to give a lot of choices. Which pajamas, which pillow, would you like to brush your teeth first or put on your pajamas first? Do you want a story? If it were totally up to my kids, they would watch movies in the living room until they passed out well past midnight every night. They cannot be totally in charge of bedtime, but I will drag in the bean bag chairs because they decide to sleep on the floor. I try to employ as much autonomy as I can.

Sometimes, at school, kids are more or less unattended. Playgrounds and school busses are two of these places. Kids are often unkind to each other, and sometimes put their hands on someone else. In these situations, who is blamed? Is the victim being asked to simply shake it off? Is the kid doing the hitting or teasing warned that this is inappropriate? I suppose there are those who would say I am over reacting, but I think the way we respond to these first instances will tell our kids whether or not they should bother reporting other things. We need to show our kids that it is important that everyone is in charge of their own body, that it is important enough we will step in when this paradigm isn't being honored.

Our jokes tell a lot about what we really think. If we are joking about how a dad needs a shotgun because his daughters are so pretty, we are teaching that the dad needs to be in charge of his daughter's body. If we are joking about how men simply cannot stop drooling over the Dallas Cowboy cheerleaders, we are letting our sons know they aren't responsible for objectifying women.

When you are watching TV or movies and someone isn't in charge of their own bodies, point it out. My mom used this little trick to teach her girls about the sexual ethics she wanted taught in her house. I asked where babies came from in the third grade, but I knew by kindergarten when a couple on TV started kissing horizontally and then the lights went out, that represented sex, and it was for married people. My mom saw those moments as an opportunity to discuss it with us. We need to do the same thing. If you see a plotline where someone is not in charge of their own body, tell your kid. Talk about it. Explain what makes you nervous about that story, and see what your kids have to say. They might surprise you!

When you are listening to the radio I am sure you can find at least one disturbing lyric between each commercial break. Point it out. Let your kids know what bothers you about the song. Sing other cheesy lyrics your kids will inevitably roll their eyes at. This may seem silly, but it is important to point out what the culture is trying to sneak into our heads so we can replace it with the idea that everyone is in charge of their own body.

One of the best ways to have conversations with your kids about things that are important, is to do their assigned reading with them. If your kid is reading To Kill a Mockingbird for her eighth grade language arts class, then so are you. That book alone opens the conversation to the difference between consensual and nonconsensual sexual behavior (not to mention the awesome conversations about systemic racism you can have!). As a High School English teacher, I know that we deal with some pretty adult material via the books we read. But I promise, I have never brought anything up in class my students were not already talking about. Take these opportunities to teach the things you want to teach before anyone else can. Explain these books in the context of everyone getting to be in charge of their own bodies.

When your kid messes up there will be opportunities to teach that everyone is in charge of their own body. Being in charge of your own body means being in charge of your own consequences. If a kid gets mad and knocks something over, they should have to clean it up. At our house, if you cannot keep your body from hurting someone else you have to be removed from the situation and contained in your room until you can gain control of your own body. If your body comes home twenty minutes late then you have deposited twenty minutes into the time bank, and I will take those twenty minutes tomorrow morning when you want to be asleep. (My mom invented the time bank. We immediately stopped making deposits and started coming home on time.) By teaching our kids that they are responsible for their consequences, we can help our kids learn to make good decisions before the consequences are life altering.

Every day there are opportunities for me to teach my kids that they are in charge of their own bodies. Sometimes I mess this up. When I do, I apologize. I explain as best I can why my behavior was wrong. I ask forgiveness, then I try to do better. My children (and my students for that matter) are much better at extending grace than I am. This allows everyone the chance to practice the paradigm, everyone is in charge of their own bodies, and empowers our kids to try it out even when we aren't there.

Don't Underestimate Teens

Teens are capable of being amazing. And they are looking for a better way. I came across the idea that everyone is in charge of their own body after I had a conversation about rape in my ninth grade classroom. I wrote the story on my blog (accidentaldevotional.com) and was blown away by the response.

I was teaching an ambiguous poem. I suppose that is the point. The best literature for me to teach is the kind that gives the kids enough to be interested in, but they still don't have a clear idea of what is going on. We spend the day looking at the poem from every angle we can find, or at least that is the plan.

That day, pretty immediately, someone in the back shot their hand up and did not wait for me to call on them. "Ms. Norman, this poem is about rape." It wasn't a question. It is rare for a fifteen-year-old to speak about anything with this kind of authority, let alone poetry. A few kids chimed in to agree with the first student and I admitted that I often read the poem that way, even if you don't have to. I was about to launch into an explanation of other ways this poem could be read.

"Ms. Norman" another kid called, "Have you heard about that rape case in Ohio? Those guys got convicted. They have to go to jail. They are going to lose their scholarships. They were going to D-1 schools!"
"Well…"I responded, feeling the heat crawl up my neck, "maybe they are going to jail for rape because THEY ARE RAPISTS!" I yelled those last three words at my kids and watched as some of them blinked in surprise. Apparently, the thought had never occurred to them that these athletes who were convicted of rape, were in fact rapists.

It is a strange thing about looking into the face of a 15-year-old, to really see who they are. You still see the small child that their mother sees. You see the man or woman they will be before they graduate. They are babies whose innocence you want desperately to protect. They are old enough to know better, even if no one has taught them.

I realized then that some of my kids were genuinely confused. "How can she be raped?" they asked, "She wasn't awake to say no." These words out of a fully-fledged adult would have made me furious. I did get a good few minutes in response on victim blaming and why it is so terrible. But out of the face of a kid who still has baby fat, those words just made me sick. My students are still young enough, that mostly they just spout what they have learned, and they have learned that absent a no, the yes is implied.

It is uncomfortable to think that some of the students you still call babies have the potential to be rapists. It is sickening, it is terrifying, but it is true. It is a reality we have to face. My students have lived in a world for fifteen years where the joke "she probably wanted it" isn't really a joke, they need to unlearn some lessons that no one will admit to teaching them. Standing in front of my classroom and stating that a woman's clothing choice is never permission to rape her should not be a radical act. But only a few heads nodded in agreement. Most were stunned, like this was a completely new thought.

The follow up questions were terrifying in their earnestness. "Ms. Norman, you mean a woman walking down the street naked is not her inviting sex? How will I know she wants to have sex?" A surprisingly bold voice came out of a girl in the back "You'll know when she says, you want to have sex?!"

If you want to keep teens from being rapists, you can no longer assume that they know how. You HAVE to talk about it. There is no longer a choice. It is no longer enough to talk to our kids about the mechanics of sex, it probably never was. We have to talk about consent, what it means, and how you are sure you have it.

What came next, when the idea of a clear yes came up, is the reason I will always choose to teach freshmen. They are still young enough to want to entertain new ideas. When we reversed the conversation from, "well she didn't say no," to "she has to say YES!" many of them lit up. "Ms. Norman," they said, "that does make a lot more sense." "Ms. Norman," they exclaimed, "that way leaves a lot less confusion." When one of the boys asked, well what do you want me to do, get a napkin and make her sign it, about four girls from the back yelled, YEAH!

In the span of one conversation we found a better way, and everyone got behind it. Our kids know that things aren't right as they are. They want the world to be better. *They* want to be better. Teaching and acting on "everyone is in charge of their own bodies" gives our teens a world that is safer, where no one gets confused and everyone gets a say in what happens to them. We owe this to the, we owe this to ourselves. We can do better. Let's start today. Everyone is in charge of their own body.

About the Author

Photo by Jennifer Upton

Abby thrives on distributing complex ideas to the masses. As a teacher, Abby began her career in one of the most underserved areas of the country. There she discovered her voice in the classroom as she explored concepts like race, gender and social justice through the literature her students were reading. She is sure she learned more than she taught. Her students showed her that most people are interested in engaging and improving the world if they are just given the words to explore it

Abby believes in champagne for celebrating everyday life, laughing until her stomach hurts and telling the truth, even when it is hard, maybe especially then. You can find her blogging at accidentaldevotional.com and tweeting at @accidentaldevo. Or just email her at accidentaldevotional@gmail.com. Abby loves all kinds of Girl Scout cookies and literally burning lies in her backyard fire pit.

83807858R00020

Made in the USA
Lexington, KY
16 March 2018